How
DINOSAURS
Came to Be

How
DINOSAURS
Came to Be

Written by Patricia Lauber
Illustrated by Douglas Henderson

SIMON & SCHUSTER BOOKS FOR YOUNG READERS

Also by Patricia Lauber

DINOSAURS WALKED HERE
AND OTHER STORIES FOSSILS TELL

LIVING WITH DINOSAURS

THE NEWS ABOUT DINOSAURS

VOLCANO:
THE ERUPTION AND HEALING
OF MOUNT ST. HELENS

The author would like to thank Dr. Donald Baird,
Director Emeritus of the Museum of Natural History at Princeton University,
for his thoughtful comments and generous help.

To illustrate *How Dinosaurs Came to Be*, Douglas Henderson used a variety of
drawing media, including pastel, ink, watercolor, and stone lithography.

SIMON & SCHUSTER BOOKS FOR YOUNG READERS
An imprint of Simon & Schuster Children's Publishing Division
1230 Avenue of the Americas, New York, New York 10020

Text copyright © 1996 by Patricia Lauber
Illustrations copyright © 1996 by Douglas Henderson

Book design by Sylvia Frezzolini Severance
The text for this book is set in 13.5 Sabon.
Manufactured in the United States of America
First Edition

10 9 8 7 6 5 4 3 2 1

Library of Congress Cataloging-in-Publication Data
Lauber, Patricia. How dinosaurs came to be / by Patricia Lauber;
illustrated by Douglas Henderson. — 1st ed.   p. cm. Includes index.
ISBN 0-689-80531-4
1. Dinosaurs — Juvenile literature. 2. Evolution (Biology) —Juvenile literature.
[1. Dinosaurs. 2. Prehistoric animals. 3. Evolution.] I. Henderson, Douglas, ill. II. Title.
QE862.D5L456 1996
567.9'1—dc20   94-6667

❧ CONTENTS ❧

CHAPTER ONE

The World of the Early Dinosaurs

The lizard is running for its life. Tail held off the ground, it streaks for shelter, hoping to hide. But it is no match for the hungry dinosaur. Sprinting on long legs, the dinosaur overtakes and seizes the lizard. Its jaws open. They are lined with sharp teeth, each edged like a steak knife.

The hunter is *Coelophysis*, and it is one of the early dinosaurs. Like the others, it is a meat-eater that walks and runs on its hind legs. Its short front legs are used for seizing and tearing prey apart. *Coelophysis* is fairly small—3 feet high and 8 feet long—but built for speed. It eats whatever it can catch. If hungry enough, it may even eat young of its own kind.

Coelophysis first appeared about 230 million years ago, in a time called the Middle Triassic. It roamed upland forests, often hunting in packs near lakes and streams. From time to time, it may have gone for a swim to cool off. The world's climate was much warmer then than it is now. But *Coelophysis* must have approached the water with caution.

Metoposaurus was a 10-foot-long amphibian, an animal that can live both in the water and on land.

Giant meat-eating amphibians, called metoposaurs, lurked in the mud of lakes and streams, waiting to sink their teeth in any creature that came near their jaws. Phytosaurs, reptiles that looked like crocodiles, were ready to gobble down metoposaurs and dinosaurs, as well as fish.

Rutiodon was a 10-foot-long phytosaur.

In the Middle Triassic, the land swarmed with reptiles of all sizes, shapes, and kinds—from dinosaurs to lizards. Waddling, scuttling, striding, the reptiles went about their business. Plant-eaters munched ferns and mosses or chomped on seeds and fruits. Meat-eaters lay in wait or chased their prey. Grunts and growls mingled with the sound of wind in the trees or the pounding torrents of rain that fell from time to time. This was the world of the early dinosaurs.

We know about these ancient times through fossils. These are traces of plants and animals that were buried in sand or other material that later hardened into layers of rock.

The study of fossils is called paleontology. The scientists who study them are paleontologists. When these scientists find different animals in the same layers of rock, they know that the animals lived at the same time. Traces of plants are clues to what some of the animals ate. They are also clues to what the climate was like.

Fossils form a record of life on earth, and they show that life is always changing. Some kinds of life die out and disappear from the fossil record. New kinds appear. Now and then, there is a great dying out—a mass extinction—after which many new kinds appear.

By studying the fossil record, paleontologists can see when and how new kinds of life developed. They see, for example, that dinosaurs first appeared in the Middle Triassic. Where did dinosaurs come from? The fossil record gives the answer—it shows the direct ancestors of dinosaurs. These were reptiles that lived in the Early Triassic and in an earlier period called the Permian. All the dinosaurs we know developed from these reptiles.

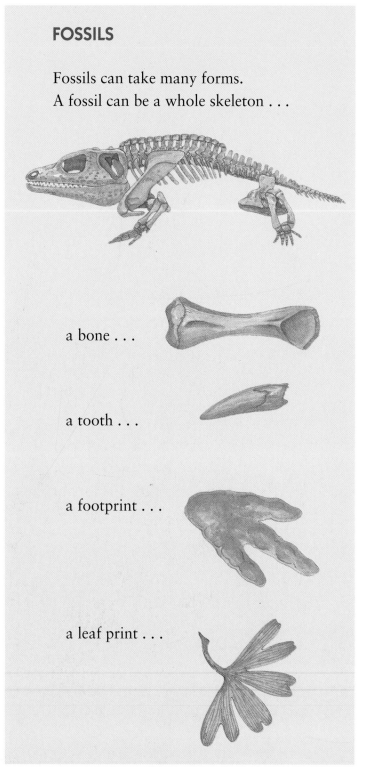

FOSSILS

Fossils can take many forms.
A fossil can be a whole skeleton . . .

a bone . . .

a tooth . . .

a footprint . . .

a leaf print . . .

The same fossil record shows something else that's interesting. Still other reptiles of the Permian and the Triassic became the ancestors of mammals. And for a time the mammal ancestors were much more successful than the dinosaur ancestors. It almost seemed as if there might never be dinosaurs, as if they would never have a chance to develop. But as everybody knows, dinosaurs did develop, ruling the land for millions of years. How all of this happened is the story in this book.

TIME SCALE

ERA	PERIOD	APPROXIMATE NUMBER OF YEARS AGO PERIOD BEGAN
CENOZOIC ERA	Quaternary Period	2 million—continues to present
CENOZOIC ERA	Tertiary Period	65 million
MESOZOIC ERA	Cretaceous Period	144 million
MESOZOIC ERA	Jurassic Period	213 million
MESOZOIC ERA	Triassic Period	248 million
PALEOZOIC ERA	Permian Period	286 million

Fossils show that during the earth's long history, many kinds of plants and animals have appeared. All developed from earlier kinds of plants and animals. Most lived for millions of years, then disappeared. New kinds of life took their place, lived, died out, and left their fossils.

Scientists use this fossil record to divide the earth's history into units. Each unit stands for a time when particular groups of plants and animals lived.

The biggest units are called eras. Each era is made up of several smaller units called periods. Periods, in turn, may be made up of still smaller units called epochs.

The Permian, for example, is the last period in the Paleozoic (Ancient Life) Era. The Triassic is the first period in the Mesozoic (Middle Life) Era.

This chart shows some of the units in the earth's history and tells how many million years ago each began.

CHAPTER TWO

Big Changes During the Permian

The morning sun has cleared the trees. It streams down on the shore of a lake, where some big-bodied, 10-foot-long reptiles are sprawled. Like all reptiles, they must warm up before they can be active.

Each has a sail, or fin, on its back. The sail is an arc of bony spines covered with skin. It gives an animal extra body surface—more body to soak up heat. The sun-warmed blood in the sail helps to heat the rest of the body. Reptiles with sails will be up and about before many others. The sails give them a head start.

These animals are pelycosaurs. They are reptiles that were ancestors of mammals, and so they are sometimes called mammal-like reptiles. The ones sunning themselves by the lake are meat-eaters named *Dimetrodon*.

Edaphosaurus

Their plant-eating relatives, 10-foot-long *Edaphosaurus,* also have sails, although many other pelycosaurs do not.

Pelycosaurs lived during the Permian, a time when the earth was home to many kinds of reptiles and amphibians. One big amphibian lives in the lake near *Dimetrodon.* This is *Eryops,* 6 feet long with a bulky body and short, thick legs. Much of its time is spent resting on the lake bottom. Only its eyes move as it waits for a meal to pass by. It eats almost any kind of fish, among them small freshwater sharks.

In the Early Permian, reptiles and amphibians lived in regions along the equator. Here the climate had been warm and wet for millions of years, just right for both of them. But the Permian was a period that saw a big change in the face of the earth, which brought about big changes in climate. Very slowly, earth's land masses were moving together. By the Late Permian, they had collided and formed one huge continent, called Pangaea, a name that means "all earth."

On land, *Eryops* waddled along on short legs.

CONTINENTS ON THE MOVE

The earth has a solid outer shell that is divided into big pieces called plates. The plates are always in motion. Very slowly they are carried about by currents of molten rock that rise from inside the earth. The currents rise, spread sideways, cool, then turn down, back into the earth. Earth's land masses ride the plates like passengers on rafts.

If currents rise under a land mass, they tear it apart. But there are also times when currents bring land masses together, when continents collide.

In the Early Permian, the earth had two big continents. By the Late Permian, these had collided. The earth had just one huge continent: Pangaea.

Much later Pangaea would break up. Smaller land masses would move apart and in time become the continents we know.

EARLY PERMIAN

LATE PERMIAN

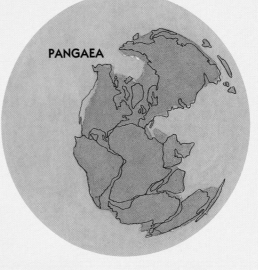

Present-day continents are shown with solid lines.

Land that had been near the South Pole was carried north and warmed up. Ice melted, and green plants took hold.

Where the two continents collided, their edges crumpled into mountains. Volcanoes erupted.

Climates changed. Mountains cut off rain-bearing winds, and swamps became deserts. Torrents of rain fell in once-dry areas. Regions near the equator began to have seasons—a hot, dry season and a hot, wet season. In dry seasons, ponds, streams, and small lakes dried up.

These great changes in climate took place over thousands and thousands of years. Some plants and animals were able to change, to adapt. Others could not.

Many big amphibians died out when their lakes and streams dried up. But some small amphibians were able to burrow into mud, sleep through a dry season, and wake when the rains came again.

Cacops

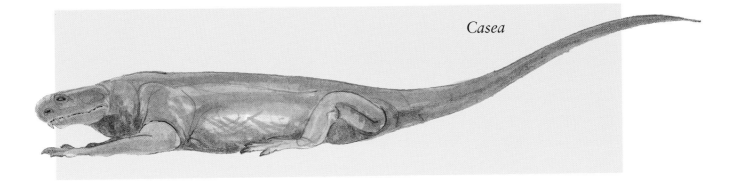

Casea

For some animals, change offered a chance to spread into uplands, higher areas that had earlier been too cold for amphibians and reptiles.

Cacops, for example, was a small amphibian, just 16 inches long, that could live in a drier world, as could its relatives. Their bodies were armored with bony plates that kept their skin from drying out in sun and wind. Good at walking, these animals could reach new areas easily. They probably lived near upland streams, since amphibians must lay their eggs in water.

Small reptiles also moved into newly warm areas, where they fed on insects, spiders, millipedes, centipedes, and other small creatures. They were joined by plant-eating reptiles, such as *Casea,* a 4-foot-long pelycosaur that ate ferns and horsetails, and the biggest pelycosaur of all, 13-foot-long *Cotylorhynchus.*

Cotylorhynchus

Sphenacodon

Meat-eaters followed the plant-eaters. *Dimetrodon* may have feasted on plant-eating pelycosaurs. So may *Sphenacodon,* a 10-foot-long relative. Like *Dimetrodon, Sphenacodon* had huge jaws armed with three kinds of teeth—incisors in front for biting food, canines for ripping and tearing, and cheek teeth for cutting. These meat-eaters were the world's top predators—big enough and strong enough to eat any other animal they met.

Pelycosaurs were successful animals. By the Middle Permian, nearly three-quarters of all land animals were pelycosaurs. They were big and small, plant-eaters and meat-eaters. Some had sails, some did not. Yet all had developed, through small changes, from a group of reptiles that looked like 20-inch-long lizards.

Small changes are likely to occur in any group. A few young animals, for example, may have longer legs than their parents or teeth that are slightly different.

Some changes are helpful. Longer legs help the young to move faster. New tooth shapes let animals eat new kinds of food or simply chew better. The young become more successful than animals without the changes. They get more food, live longer, and have more young. They pass on the changes to their own young.

Over time, small changes can add up to big ones. An animal that swallowed chunks of meat may have descendants that eat only plants. An animal that waddled may have descendants that walk upright. And so, in time, a new kind of animal appears. It has branched off from an earlier kind.

By studying the fossil record, paleontologists can see pelycosaurs growing bigger and heavier. They see stronger jaws. They see teeth of different sizes and shapes, suited to eating meat, plants, or insects.

During the Permian, paleontologists also see a new group of animals branching off from the pelycosaur family to which *Dimetrodon* and *Sphenacodon* belonged. These animals were the therapsids. By the Late Permian, these mammal-like reptiles ruled the land, taking the place of the pelycosaurs.

A great dying out brought the Permian to a close. It was the biggest mass extinction in earth's history. No one knows what caused it, but the best guess is a change in climate that came as Pangaea moved.

Many, many kinds of animals disappeared forever from the land and seas. Among them were the biggest therapsids. But smaller therapsids lived on into the Triassic, and they were becoming more and more like mammals.

CHAPTER THREE

Therapsids and Mammals

The afternoon sun is a yellow ball near the horizon. Shadows grow long. Where the sun warms a bare spot of hillside, three young animals are playing. Their mother is nearby. From some distance away, she looks like a small, stocky dog. Seen closer up, she doesn't really look like a mammal, but she doesn't look like a reptile either. For one thing, she has no scales covering her skin.

This animal is *Thrinaxodon,* a mammal-like reptile of the Early Triassic. *Thrinaxodon* was an advanced therapsid, one that was more like a mammal than a reptile. Probably it had fur and was warm-blooded. Early therapsids were cold-blooded.

Cold-blooded animals cannot make their own heat and keep a steady body temperature. They warm up by sunning themselves. They cool off by moving into shade or water. Until a reptile has warmed up, it is sluggish. Its energy comes from the sun's heat, from outside its body.

Lycaenops was only 3 feet long and lightly built, with long legs made for running. It probably hunted in packs and preyed on plant-eating therapsids, such as *Moschops*.

Warm-blooded animals do make their own heat and keep a steady body temperature. They can be active by day and by night. Many can live in cool or cold places. Their energy comes from their food, from the way food is digested and used inside their bodies.

To keep up their body heat, warm-blooded animals must eat more

Moschops was big—16 feet long, with a heavy body and a large head. Its front legs sprawled sideways, but its hind legs were more directly under the body. This therapsid bit off food with its chisel-shaped front teeth. It may have defended itself from meat-eaters by butting them with its head.

than cold-blooded animals do and they must eat more often. Their bodies must digest food faster and use it faster.

Paleontologists cannot study the insides of therapsids, because soft body parts rotted away millions of years ago. But fossils offer clues to changes that made therapsids more and more like mammals.

Unlike early therapsids, *Thrinaxodon* walked like a mammal. All four legs were beneath its body. Its feet pointed forward. It could move easily and swiftly, in long strides.

Bones in the jaws and skull had changed. Advanced therapsids had stronger jaw muscles—and a stronger bite. They had better hearing and a better sense of smell.

Thrinaxodon could take deeper breaths than early therapsids. Its rib cage was short and closed off by a sheet of muscle that helped the lungs work. The lungs sent more oxygen into the bloodstream. The oxygen speeded up digestion. It let *Thrinaxodon* run longer distances.

Still other changes made it possible to chew and breathe at the same time without choking. Therapsids could take in oxygen while chewing up their food.

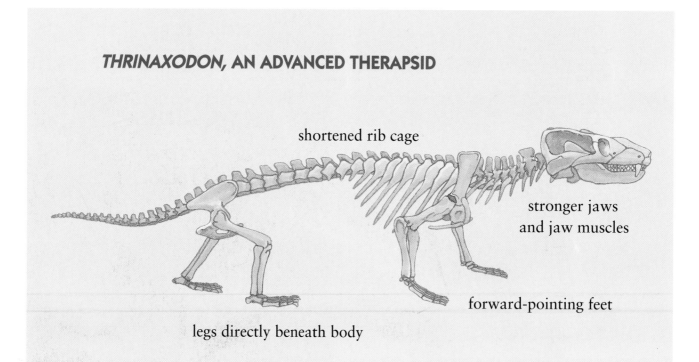

THRINAXODON, AN ADVANCED THERAPSID

shortened rib cage

stronger jaws and jaw muscles

forward-pointing feet

legs directly beneath body

Kannemeyeria grew to be 10 feet long, with a thick body and a huge head. Instead of teeth, it had a horny beak with which it tore off mouthfuls of leaves and roots, grinding them up between its toothless jaws.

Lystrosaurus, another plant-eater, was about 3 feet long. It lived the way a hippo does today, wallowing in shallow water or resting on the shore. Its nostrils and eyes were placed far back on the skull. They stayed above water while *Lystrosaurus* floated or swam with its body underwater. This therapsid had tusks and a beak like a turtle's that was powered by strong jaw muscles.

Thrinaxodon belonged to the most successful group, which existed for 80 million years, from the Late Permian to the Middle Jurassic. Mammals branched off from this group.

Oligokyphus, a small plant-eater, belonged to the only family of therapsids to live into the Jurassic. It looked like a weasel, but had incisors like a beaver's. It must have gnawed off food, then chopped the food up with its cheek teeth.

Cynognathus was one of the largest members of this group. About 3 feet long, it was a fierce predator, with strong jaws and sharp teeth. Built for running, it had strong hind legs placed directly under its body.

Massetognathus was a plant-eater, about 19 inches long. Its teeth show that it was good at chewing up food, which it could keep at the back of the mouth while grinding it up.

Successful animals, therapsids lived all over Pangaea, often in climates where other reptiles could not live. Their numbers grew. New kinds appeared.

In the Early Triassic, therapsids were rulers of the land. To look at the fossil record, anyone might guess that they would go on ruling until the first mammals appeared. After that, mammals would rule the land, taking what they wanted as food and living space.

But that did not happen. By the Middle Triassic, therapsids were few in number and small in size. And when the first mammals appeared in the Late Triassic, they were not about to rule the land. They were tiny animals, the size of shrews and meadow mice. They had branched off from the group of therapsids to which *Thrinaxodon* belonged.

For millions of years, tiny mammals would scurry about the earth, peering down from trees, burrowing under the litter of forest floors to escape notice—and being eaten. They may even have hidden by day and come out at night to feed on insects and other small creatures.

Paleontologists are not sure what happened to stop therapsids and mammals from advancing. But they think the answer may lie in the climate, which kept warming during the Triassic. One idea is that the Triassic may have been too hot for animals that were warm-blooded. Perhaps, some scientists say, therapsids and early mammals had not developed ways of dealing with heat. Perhaps they did not pant or sweat. If so, it was helpful to be small. An animal with a small body loses heat much more quickly than an animal with a large body.

Whatever happened, the time was right for another group of animals. These were the thecodonts, the direct ancestors of dinosaurs.

TWO EARLY MAMMALS

The earliest known mammals appeared in the Late Triassic. Some were meat-eaters that hunted insects, caterpillars, and perhaps small reptiles. Some were plant-eaters. Many kinds developed over the years.

Megazostrodon (lower left) was one of the earliest. About 5 inches long, it looked like a shrew and, like a shrew, probably spent most of its waking hours hunting and eating. It lived from the Late Triassic to the Early Jurassic. *Haramiya, (upper right)* also 5 inches long, lived in the same time. A plant-eater, it crushed its food between its cheek teeth.

CHAPTER FOUR

Dinosaurs-in-the-Making

The animal looks like a tiny, nimble dinosaur, about 12 inches long. It darts around a rock and under a fern. Its head shoots forward and its jaws snap shut, but the insect escapes. The hunt goes on as the animal races about. From time to time, it hears a rustle of leaves. It stops, stands on its hind legs, and looks around. The sound may tell of an insect—or it may tell of a predator waiting to pounce.

The animal is not a dinosaur, but it is a close relative. It is *Lagosuchus,* an advanced thecodont of the Triassic.

The earliest thecodonts appeared in the Late Permian. One was *Chasmatosaurus,* which looked like a 6-foot-long crocodile, with sprawling legs and long jaws lined with sharp teeth. It lived in swamps, lakes, and rivers, and it preyed on fish.

Chasmatosaurus

Many early thecodonts survived the mass extinction of the Permian. And during the Triassic, thecodonts spread across the earth, taking over the living places of therapsids.

Most were meat-eaters that walked on all-fours. The earliest waddled on sprawling legs. Later thecodonts had legs that were more directly under their bodies, and members of one group were able to run upright on two legs.

An Early Triassic Thecodont

Erythrosuchus

Erythrosuchus had a large head and powerful jaws. It lived on land and walked with its legs more directly under its body than *Chasmatosaurus*. In their day, *Erythrosuchus* and other members of its family were the biggest predators on land. They grew 15 or 16 feet long. Among the animals they ate were other thecodonts. And that, some paleontologists think, may be why some thecodonts developed body armor.

An Armored Thecodont

Desmatosuchus belonged to the group of plant-eating thecodonts. All had bulky bodies armored with plates of bone that helped protect them from meat-eaters. *Desmatosuchus* also had two long spines that grew from its shoulders. This thecodont was about 16 feet long, with a small head, a snout like a pig's, and teeth like pegs.

Desmatosuchus

A Strange Thecodont

Only 6 inches long, *Longisquama* spent much of its time in trees. Its body was covered with small scales, and a row of tall scales rose from its back. Perhaps the tall scales attracted mates or were used for gliding from tree branch to tree branch. Perhaps they helped *Longisquama* soak up the sun's warmth and also gave off body heat. Perhaps they were an early stage in the development of feathers. No one knows.

Longisquama

A Jurassic Thecodont

Protosuchus looked like a 5-foot long crocodile. It preyed on land animals and on fish.

Protosuchus

Three Dinosaur-like Thecodonts

Euparkeria was 2 feet long and slim, with a large head and sharp cutting teeth. Its strong hind legs were longer than its front legs. Although it spent most of its time on four legs, it could rise up and run on its hind legs. When sprinting after prey, *Euparkeria* held its front legs back along its sides and snatched the prey with its jaws.

About 13 feet long, *Ornithosuchus* looked even more like a dinosaur, with a tyrannosaur-shaped head. Although it probably traveled on all-fours, it could walk and run on its hind legs.

Euparkeria

Ornithosuchus

Lagosuchus is the most likely ancestor of the dinosaurs—and perhaps of the pterosaurs, the flying reptiles that appeared in the Late Triassic. The bones of its hips, hind legs, and ankles are like those of the earliest dinosaurs.

Thecodonts lived on earth for more than 40 million years, dying out in the Late Triassic. But well before that, the first dinosaurs had branched off from them, starting the age of dinosaurs.

Lagosuchus

CHAPTER FIVE

The First Dinosaurs

Fifty or sixty small dinosaurs are trotting along on their hind legs, their long, slim tails held out for balance. Their bodies are dappled by sunlight filtering through the forest trees. Twigs snap under their feet. Somewhere nearby, plant-eaters are munching and crunching, then moving on to fresh food supplies. The dinosaurs' narrow heads twist and turn, senses alert to danger.

Arriving at a lake, they pause and look around, but no phytosaur or other big meat-eater seems to be lying in wait. They wade into the lake and, like a flock of long-legged waterbirds, start to feed on fish, snails, and insects.

The dinosaurs are *Coelophysis,* and their fossil footprints show that large numbers often moved about together. They may have hunted large prey in packs. They may have been drawn to lakes and streams, where there was food for all.

LIZARD-HIPPED AND BIRD-HIPPED

Paleontologists divide dinosaurs into two big groups.

One group has hipbones arranged like those of reptiles. They are called lizard-hipped dinosaurs, or *Saurischia*.

The other has hipbones arranged like those of birds. They are called bird-hipped dinosaurs, or *Ornithischia*.

Both groups may have developed from thecodonts. Or the bird-hipped dinosaurs may have developed from lizard-hipped dinosaurs. No one is sure. But paleontologists do know that the earliest dinosaurs to walk the earth were lizard-hipped meat-eaters. They appeared some 230 million years ago, in the Middle Triassic.

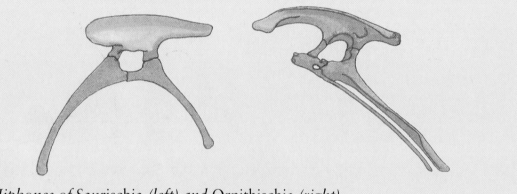

Hipbones of Saurischia *(left) and* Ornithischia *(right).*

Some Early Lizard-hipped Dinosaurs

Coelophysis belonged to the group of lizard-hipped dinosaurs that walked erect on two legs and ate meat. A second group of lizard-hipped dinosaurs walked on all-fours and ate plants.

The meat-eaters appeared first, and they looked and lived much like thecodonts. They were fast runners, with slender necks and long tails. Their arms were shorter than their legs and were used for grasping prey or carrying food to their mouths.

Eoraptor

So far, the very first dinosaurs have not been discovered. But of all the earliest known dinosaurs, *Eoraptor* is the most primitive, the one closest to the thecodonts. About the size of a dog, it was 3 feet long from nose to tip of tail and weighed about 25 pounds. It used its long fingers and claws for raking meat from its prey.

Procompsognathus was a small, speedy dinosaur, about 4 feet in length. Running on long legs, it chased after lizards and insects.

Procompsognathus

Herrerasaurus

    Herrerasaurus belonged to a group that branched off from the first dinosaurs. Ten to 20 feet long, it weighed 300 to 450 pounds. Its jaws and hands show that it was a fearsome animal.

    Saltopus was one of the smallest and lightest dinosaurs. About 2 feet long, it weighed only 2 pounds. It, too, chased after lizards, insects, and other small prey.

Saltopus

Coelophysis

Coelophysis was bigger, reaching 8 to 10 feet in length and weighing up to 50 pounds. As well as eating lizards and fish, it may have preyed on plant-eating dinosaurs.

No one is sure whether the earliest plant-eaters branched off from the thecodonts or from the early meat-eating dinosaurs. But many of the plant-eaters probably looked like *Anchisaurus*, with a small head at the end of a long neck. The arms of this dinosaur were shorter than its legs, but it probably walked on all-fours most of the time. When feeding, it balanced on two legs and used its long fingers to gather plants and leaves. It was about 7 feet long.

Anchisaurus

Massospondylus

Massospondylus was twice as long, with hands that could be used for walking or gathering food. It ate tough plants and swallowed rough stones to help break down its food, just as some birds do today. Stones, polished from use, have been found with the dinosaur's bones.

Plateosaurus

Plateosaurus was still bigger, reaching a length of 23 feet. It may have moved about in herds, searching for new feeding grounds. Although this dinosaur traveled on all-fours, it could stand on its hind legs and reach up to browse on the leaves of trees.

Some Early Bird-hipped Dinosaurs

All the bird-hipped dinosaurs were plant-eaters. Paleontologists divide them into four big groups. Three groups walked on all-fours. The fourth, and earliest, group walked on two legs. Only a few of the two-legged bird-hipped dinosaurs had appeared by the Late Triassic.

Among them were the family called fabrosaurs. These were small animals, 2 to 4 feet long, that ran on long, slim legs. They looked much like the small lizard-hipped meat-eaters.

Lesothosaurus was a fabrosaur. It had a small head with a rather flat face. Its teeth were shaped like arrowheads and spaced apart, so that the upper teeth fitted between the lower ones when the dinosaur chewed. They were teeth that could chop up tough plant food. *Lesothosaurus* was lightly built and had long legs that must have carried it swiftly over the hot dry plains where it lived.

Lesothosaurus

Scutellosaurus was 4 feet long and is the only armored fabrosaur known. Rows of bony studs covered its back and sides. Because its arms were longer than those of other fabrosaurs, scientists think that *Scutellosaurus* rested on all-fours when browsing.

Scutellosaurus

Heterodontosaurus

Heterodontosaurus belonged to another early family. Members of this family looked like fabrosaurs and were also small. But they had teeth unlike those of any other dinosaur. The front of the mouth had teeth only in the upper jaw, and they were small and pointed. The front of the lower jaw was a horny beak. *Heterodontosaurus* nipped off plant food with its teeth and beak and ground the food up with teeth in the back of its mouth. This group of dinosaurs was the first to have cheeks. Cheeks were useful, because they kept food from falling out of the mouth when a dinosaur was chewing.

The first dinosaurs appeared during the Middle Triassic. Thriving, they grew in numbers and kinds and lived all over Pangaea. By the Late Triassic, when the first mammals appeared, dinosaurs ruled the land. Then another mass extinction took place, and the Triassic came to an end. Many kinds of animals died out. But among those that survived into the Jurassic were dinosaurs, therapsids, and early mammals.

During the Jurassic, the last of the therapsids died out. The mammals lived on, scurrying about in the undergrowth of forests, almost invisible in the world of dinosaurs.

In the millions of years to come, in a world climate that was warm and even hot, hundreds of kinds of dinosaurs would develop. These years were not a good time to be a mammal, but they were clearly a splendid time to be a dinosaur.

⤊ INDEX ⤋

Illustration references are in **boldface type**